The Christian and the Law

Malcolm Webber

Published by:

Strategic Press
www.StrategicPress.org

Strategic Press is a division of Strategic Global Assistance, Inc.
www.sgai.org

513 S. Main St. Suite 2
Elkhart, IN 46516
U.S.A.

+1-844-532-3371 (LEADER-1)

Copyright © 2002 Malcolm Webber

ISBN 978-1-888810-59-2

All Scripture references are from the New International Version of the Bible, unless otherwise noted.

Printed in the United States of America

Contents

Introduction 5

1. Why Study the Law? 7
2. What is the Law? 11
3. The Law of Moses 17
4. Why was the Law Given? 29
5. Jesus' Relationship to the Law 41
6. The Cross and the Law 45
7. The Christian and the Law 49
8. New Life in Christ 57
9. Legalism 71
10. The Appropriate Use of the Law 77
11. Jewish Believers and the Law 83
12. Specific Issues 87

Appendix:
    Key Differences between Law and Grace 101

Introduction

A systematic study of the law may seem to be dry and academic. In reality, such a study is enormously interesting with profound practical consequences.

Paul labored over this subject so that the church could have a clear understanding of the nature both of the law and of the Christian's relationship to the law.

Unfortunately, in today's church there is more confusion on the matter than comprehension.

Consequently, this book may contain teachings that contradict some of what you have been taught before. As you read, we ask two things:

- Please study this whole book before coming to final conclusions about any one part of it.
- Please put the teachings of the Bible before human traditions.

Our hope is that this small volume will bring light and clarity to the vital issue of the Christian's relationship to the law.

Malcolm Webber, Ph.D.
Elkhart, Indiana
October 2002

Why Study the Law?

There are at least three reasons why a study of the Christian and the law is necessary.

A Central Place in Scripture

First, the law has a central place in the Scriptures. Consider the words of Jesus:

> *Do not think that I have come to abolish the Law or the Prophets; I have not come to abolish them but to fulfill them. I tell you the truth, until heaven and earth disappear, not the smallest letter, not the least stroke of a pen, will by any means disappear from the Law until everything is accomplished. (Matt. 5:17-18)*

Jesus did not denigrate the law; He commended it! Paul also praised the law:

> So then, the law is holy, and the commandment is holy, righteous and good. (Rom. 7:12)

> ...I agree that the law is good. (Rom. 7:16; cf. Deut. 4:8; Neh. 9:13; Acts 7:38)

Other than matters directly relating to Jesus Christ Himself, few topics receive more extensive treatment by Paul than does the law. Thus, to misunderstand or neglect the law is to misunderstand or neglect a large portion of the Word of God.

Necessary for Salvation

Second, a right relationship to the law is necessary for salvation.

> ...Stand firm, then, and do not let yourselves be burdened again by a yoke of slavery. Mark my words! I, Paul, tell you that if you let yourselves be circumcised, Christ will be of no value to you at all. Again I declare to every man who lets himself be circumcised that he is obligated to obey the whole law. You who are trying to be justified by law have been alienated from Christ; you have fallen away from grace... (Gal. 5:1-4)

According to Paul, when a person tries to be justified before God through keeping the law, he has become "alienated from Christ" and has "fallen away from grace"! Certainly this means he is not saved. Thus, the Christian must have a right relationship to the law – at least regarding the major issues. It is necessary for eternal life!

Much Confusion

Third, many Christians are confused about the law. This is because there is much wrong teaching on the subject. Areas of common misunderstanding include the following:

1. Were the Israelites in the Old Testament saved through keeping the law?

2. Is the Christian under the Law of Moses in any sense? Perhaps we are free from having to keep the ceremonial and civil parts of the law, but are we still obligated to keep the moral law, the Ten Commandments?

3. Is the Christian supposed to keep the Jewish feasts, the Sabbath or other religious observances?

4. If the Christian is not under the law, then are we free to break the law?

These and other questions trouble the minds of many believers.

To begin with, let's establish the meaning of the term "the law" in the Bible.

What is the Law?

The word "law" is used in the Bible more than 500 times (about 300 times in the Old Testament and over 200 in the New). It can refer to:

- The Old Testament in general.
- The Pentateuch.
- The Law of Moses.
- The Ten Commandments.

In every case, a study of the context will determine which meaning is in view.

The Old Testament

First, "the law" can refer to the Old Testament in general.

In John 12:34, when the people said, "We have heard from the Law that the Christ will remain forever," they meant the Scriptures of the Old Testament referring to such Messianic passages as Psalm 89:28-29, Psalm 110:4, Daniel 2:44 and Daniel 7:13-14.

In Romans 3:19, when Paul says, "Now we know that whatever the law says, it says to those who are under the law," he refers to the law in the general sense of the Old Testament revelation since the string of quotations he just gave (vv. 10-18) is drawn from various parts of the Old Testament, including the psalms and the prophets.

Consider also Paul's words in 1 Corinthians 14:

> In the Law it is written: "Through men of strange tongues and through the lips of foreigners I will speak to this people, but even then they will not listen to me," says the Lord. (1 Cor. 14:21)

This is a direct quote from Isaiah 28:11-12.

The Pentateuch

Second, "the law" can refer to the Pentateuch, the first five books of the Old Testament.

People commonly think of the Old Testament as a book of law. Indeed, the Old Testament does contain 613 commandments to Israel. However, only four of the thirty-nine Old Testament books contain these laws: Exodus, Leviticus, Numbers and Deuteronomy. These books, along with Genesis, were all written by Moses and are often referred to as "the law." They are also called the "Pentateuch," which means a volume consisting of five books or sections.

> *Tell me, ye that desire to be under the law, do ye not hear the law? For it is written, that Abraham had two sons, the one by a bondmaid, the other by a freewoman. (Gal. 4:21-22)*

Paul tells the Galatians to "hear the law" and proceeds to recount a story from Genesis.

The Jews call the Old Testament, "The Law, the Prophets and the Writings" (cf. Luke 24:44). The law, thus referred to, consists of the Pentateuch.

The Law of Moses

Third, "the law" can refer to the Mosaic Covenant or the "Law of Moses."

> *For the law was given through Moses; grace and truth came through Jesus Christ. (John 1:17)*

This was the revelation that God gave Moses of the covenant relationship between Himself and the nation of Israel. This covenant set Israel apart from the other nations (Ex. 19:3-6; 20:1-17; 21:1ff; Deut. 26:16-19).

God's covenant with Israel is called the "Mosaic Covenant" since it was given through Moses. It is also described as "the law" around which it revolved. Another term used is the "Sinaitic Covenant" since it was made at Mt. Sinai (Lev. 26:46). In a special sense it is also referred to as the "Old Covenant" (2 Cor. 3:14; Heb. 8:6) when compared with the "New Covenant" in Jesus Christ.

This is the way that the expression "the law" is used most frequently in both testaments. For example:

Afterward, Joshua read all the words of the law – the blessings and the curses – just as it is written in the Book of the Law. There was not a word of all that Moses had commanded that Joshua did not read to the whole assembly of Israel, including the women and children, and the aliens who lived among them. (Josh. 8:34-35)

Yet he did not put the sons of the assassins to death, in accordance with what is written in the Book of the Law of Moses where the Lord commanded: "Fathers shall not be put to death for their children, nor children put to death for their fathers; each is to die for his own sins." (2 Kings 14:6)

Then Jeshua son of Jozadak and his fellow priests and Zerubbabel son of Shealtiel and his associates began to build the altar of the God of Israel to sacrifice burnt offerings on it, in accordance with what is written in the Law of Moses the man of God. (Ezra 3:2)

All Israel has transgressed your law and turned away, refusing to obey you. Therefore the curses and sworn judgments written in the Law of Moses, the servant of God, have been poured out on us, because we have sinned against you. (Dan. 9:11)

Put the trumpet to your lips! An eagle is over the house of the Lord because the people have broken my covenant and rebelled against my law. (Hos. 8:1)

Through him everyone who believes is justified from everything you could not be justified from by the Law of Moses. (Acts 13:39)

Then some of the believers who belonged to the party of the Pharisees stood up and said, "The Gentiles must be circumcised and required to obey the Law of Moses." (Acts 15:5)

> *For it is written in the Law of Moses: "Do not muzzle an ox while it is treading out the grain."... (1 Cor. 9:9, with Deut. 25:4)*

> *Anyone who rejected the Law of Moses died without mercy on the testimony of two or three witnesses. (Heb. 10:28)*

The Ten Commandments

Fourth, "the law" can also refer to the Ten Commandments (Ex. 20:1-17).

> *The LORD said to Moses, "Come up to me on the mountain and stay here, and I will give you the tablets of stone, with the law and commands I have written for their instruction." (Ex. 24:12)*

On these two tablets of stone were written the Ten Commandments.

> *When the LORD finished speaking to Moses on Mount Sinai, he gave him the two tablets of the Testimony, the tablets of stone inscribed by the finger of God. (Ex. 31:18)*

> *...And he wrote on the tablets the words of the covenant – the Ten Commandments. (Ex. 34:28)*

> *He declared to you his covenant, the Ten Commandments, which he commanded you to follow and then wrote them on two stone tablets. (Deut. 4:13; see also 10:4)*

It is significant that the Decalogue (the Ten Commandments) was not a self-contained unit that stood in isolation; it was an integral part of the whole Mosaic Law.

These are the four ways that the expression "the law" is used in the Bible; the context will determine this. However, as we have noted, the expression is most commonly used to refer to the Law of Moses – the Mosaic Covenant between God and Israel. We will now consider the Law of Moses in detail.

The Law of Moses

There are three things we must clearly understand about the Law of Moses:

1. The Law of Moses was never intended for the Gentiles. It was only ever given to Israel.

2. The law was one single, complete system. It is quite artificial and unbiblical to break it into "sub-kinds" of law such as moral, ceremonial and civil.

3. The law was not God's permanent answer to man's need – it was only given as a temporary measure.

Only Given to Israel

First, it is important to understand that the Law of Moses was only ever given to Israel. The Mosaic Covenant was never intended for the Gentiles. The specific covenant relationship that God had with Israel has never been offered to anyone else:

> *He has revealed his word to Jacob, his laws and decrees to Israel. He has done this for no other nation; they do not know his laws. (Ps. 147:19-20)*

> *And who is like your people Israel – the one nation on earth whose God went out to redeem a people for himself, and to make a name for yourself... (1 Chron. 17:21)*

> *You only have I chosen of all the families of the earth; therefore I will punish you for all your sins. (Amos 3:2)*

> *Therefore, remember that formerly you who are Gentiles by birth and called "uncircumcised" by those who call themselves "the circumcision" (that done in the body by the hands of men) – remember that at that time you were separate from Christ, excluded from citizenship in Israel and foreigners to the covenants of the promise, without hope and without God in the world. (Eph. 2:11-2; see also Ex. 19:5-6; Lev. 20:24, 26; Deut. 4:8; 7:6-8; 10:14-15; 14:2; 2 Sam. 7:23; 1 Kings 8:53; John 4:22; Rom. 2:12; 3:2; Eph. 14-15, 19)*

Both testaments affirm that the Mosaic Covenant was made between God and Israel:

> *These are the decrees, the laws and the regulations that the LORD established on Mount Sinai between himself and the Israelites through Moses. (Lev. 26:46)*

the people of Israel. Theirs is the adoption as sons; theirs the divine glory, the covenants, the receiving of the law, the temple worship and the promises. (Rom. 9:4)

When God saves Gentiles, He does so under the *New* Covenant[1]; He does not bring them under the old Law of Moses.

For this is My blood of the new covenant, which is shed for many for the remission of sins. (Matt. 26:28, NKJV)

He has made us competent as ministers of a new covenant – not of the letter but of the Spirit; for the letter kills, but the Spirit gives life. (2 Cor. 3:6; see also Heb. 8:6-13; 9:15; 12:24)

In the eyes of God, the Gentiles were, and remain, "without law":

And unto the Jews I became as a Jew, that I might gain the Jews; to them that are under the law, as under the law, that I might gain them that are under the law; To them that are without law, as without law, (being not without law to God, but under the law to Christ,) that I might gain them that are without law. (1 Cor. 9:20-21)

All who sin apart from the law will also perish apart from the law... (Rom. 2:12)

...Gentiles... do not have the law... they do not have the law, (Rom. 2:14)

This does not mean the Gentiles are entirely "lawless" or do not have any moral responsibility before God, but simply that they were never under the Law of Moses. As Paul teaches, there is still a law written on

---

[1] Indeed, when God saves the Jews, He does so under the New Covenant (Jer. 31:31-34).

the hearts of all men and one day they will give an account to God of their moral choices:

> *Indeed, when Gentiles, who do not have the law, do by nature things required by the law, they are a law for themselves, even though they do not have the law, since they show that the requirements of the law are written on their hearts, their consciences also bearing witness, and their thoughts now accusing, now even defending them. (Rom. 2:14-15)*

By virtue of man's original creation in the image of God he has a conscience that informs him – however imperfectly, due to man's fall – with a sense of moral right and wrong.

However, the Law of Moses was only ever given to Israel. It was never given to the Gentiles. The Gentiles have never been under the Law of Moses and should not place themselves under the law in any form.

> *Now then, why do you try to test God by putting on the necks of the disciples a yoke that neither we nor our fathers have been able to bear? No! We believe it is through the grace of our Lord Jesus that we are saved, just as they are. (Acts 15:10-11; see also Rom. 6:14-15; 7:4; 10:4; Gal. 2:3-5; 4:10-11; Eph. 2:15; Col. 2:14, 16-17)*

One Single, Complete System

Second, the Law of Moses was one single, complete system.

> *For the law was given through Moses; grace and truth came through Jesus Christ. (John 1:17)*

It was not "some laws" that were given through Moses; *the law* – the whole law, complete and entire in one system – was given at one point in history through this one man.[2] Consider Paul's words in Romans:

> *for before the law was given, sin was in the world. But sin is not taken into account when there is no law. Nevertheless, death reigned from the time of Adam to the time of Moses, even over those who did not sin by breaking a command, as did Adam, who was a pattern of the one to come. (Rom. 5:13-14)*

There are two phrases here that indicate a definite period of time: "before the law was given," and "from the time of Adam to the time of Moses." God did not give Adam a system of law to keep but only a single commandment:

> *And the LORD God commanded the man, "You are free to eat from any tree in the garden; but you must not eat from the tree of the knowledge of good and evil, for when you eat of it you will surely die." (Gen. 2:16-17)*

When Adam broke this one commandment, "sin entered the world… and death through sin" (Rom. 5:12).

However, from the time of Adam's sin until the time of Moses, there was no divine system of law revealed to the human race.[3] This period of time was "before the law was given" (Rom. 5:13).

Then, "the law was given through Moses" (John 1:17). This law was a single, complete system of commandments, statutes, ordinances and judgments relating to:

---

[2] The law was affirmed and reiterated by many prophets after Moses (2 Kings 17:13).
[3] As already noted, man did have a conscience during this time (Rom. 2:14-15), but no externally-imposed, divine system of law.

- Moral laws
- Civil laws
- Dietary laws
- Feast days and holy days
- Sacrifices and offerings
- The Levitical priesthood
- The pattern of the tabernacle

All these are contained, in their entirety, within four books of the Old Testament – Exodus, Leviticus, Numbers and Deuteronomy.

Before Moses, there was no divine system of law given to humanity. After Moses, nothing further was ever added to this system of law. The law was given once and for all:

> Hear now, O Israel, the decrees and laws I am about to teach you. Follow them so that you may live and may go in and take possession of the land that the Lord, the God of your fathers, is giving you. Do not add to what I command you and do not subtract from it, but keep the commands of the Lord your God that I give you. (Deut. 4:1-2)

Thus, the Law of Moses was one single, complete system given by God to Israel during one period of time.

Because the Law of Moses was one single, complete system, every person who comes under the law as a means of righteousness is thereby obligated to observe the whole system of law in its entirety at all times without any interruption or failure. There is no option ever given in Scripture of observing certain parts of the law and omitting certain other parts. Nor is there any option of keeping the law at certain times and failing to keep it at other times. Any person who comes under the law is necessarily obligated to keep the whole law at all times. If a person breaks only one point, he has broken the whole law:

> *For whoever keeps the whole law and yet stumbles at just one point is guilty of breaking all of it. For he who said, "Do not commit adultery," also said, "Do not murder." If you do not commit adultery but do commit murder, you have become a lawbreaker. (Jam. 2:10-11; see also Gal. 3:10; 5:3)*

It is common in certain Christian teaching to divide the Law of Moses into three parts:

- The civil or judicial law, which legislated the social responsibilities of the Israelites. This part of the law is said to have applied only to Israel.
- The ceremonial law, which legislated Israel's worship. This part of the law is said to have been abolished with Christ's death on the cross.
- The moral law, found primarily in the Ten Commandments, which identified God's standards of right and wrong. This is the part of the law that the Christian is said to be under. For example, one popular theologian wrote, "The moral law that God reveals in Scripture is always binding upon us. The Christian is to…obey the moral law of God."

However, this is an artificial and unbiblical division. While the Mosaic Law certainly did contain elements that were civil, ceremonial and moral, there is no such formal division made anywhere in the Bible. In fact, quite the opposite occurs in the Old Testament; there is frequently a blending together of the three elements. Here are some examples of this mixture:

- The fourth commandment deals with the observance of the Sabbath (Ex. 20:8-11). This commandment, although included in what is commonly called the ethical or moral law (the Ten Commandments), is quite definitely ceremonial as well as moral and civil (cf. Ex. 23:12). Moreover, its violation was punishable by civil sanctions.

- In Exodus 20:26, a moral motivation is given for a ceremonial law. So, was this law "moral" or "ceremonial"?
- In Exodus 21:28-29, ceremonial food regulations are mixed up with civil laws. In addition, God defines the one who is considered morally accountable for the accident. So, were these laws "moral," "ceremonial" or "civil"?
- In Exodus 22:21, verse 25 and verses 26-27, moral motivations are given for civil laws. So, were these laws "moral" or "civil"?
- Exodus 22:29 is an example of a law that is moral (deals with greed and heart-surrender to God), ceremonial (involving offerings) and civil (occurs in a section of laws relating to social responsibilities).
- Again in Exodus 22:31, ceremonial food regulations are mixed up with civil laws. So, were these laws "ceremonial" or "civil"? Furthermore, in Exodus 22:31, a moral reason is given for this law: "You are to be my holy people."
- In Exodus 23:1-3, the laws involve both civil and moral issues.

Such examples from the law could be multiplied. Clearly it is an artificial distinction to try to break the law into separate divisions. At first hearing, the idea of this division sounds plausible but when one actually reads the law, the impracticality of such a distinction quickly becomes apparent.

The Jews themselves regarded the law as a unit. They did not acknowledge any three part division.

The law as a governing economy over God's people stands or falls as a whole system. The following statements by Paul and James could not make sense unless the law is understood as a unit.

> Again I declare to every man who lets himself be circumcised that he is obligated to obey the whole law. (Gal. 5:3)[4]

---

[4] Paul here is not condemning circumcision for medical reasons, but for reasons

For whoever keeps the whole law and yet stumbles at just one point is guilty of breaking all of it. (Jam. 2:10)

The law demands perfection in all areas as Deuteronomy 27 states:

Cursed is the man who does not uphold the words of this law by carrying them out... (Deut. 27:26)

The law is not simply a collection of various parts. It is a whole and must be kept in all its parts if it is to be considered kept at all. Like a chain, the law consists of different links, but it is still one chain, and it takes only one broken link to break the chain.

Paul quotes Deuteronomy 27:26 in Galatians:

All who rely on observing the law are under a curse, for it is written: "Cursed is everyone who does not continue to do everything written in the Book of the Law." (Gal. 3:10)

Significantly, Paul is dealing here with circumcision (a ceremonial aspect of the law) and he speaks of circumcision as being an integral part of the whole law. Paul refers to Deuteronomy 27 to make the point that if someone places himself under any part of the law, he thereby places himself under the whole law and under its curse, since no one can keep the whole law perfectly. Thus, the law cannot be split up into sections. That approach is simply not biblical. The Law of Moses was one single, complete system.

---

of securing or maintaining righteousness before God.

Temporary

Finally, the Law of Moses was intended by God to be only temporary:

> *What, then, was the purpose of the law? It was added because of transgressions until the Seed to whom the promise referred had come... (Gal. 3:19)*

The law "was added...until..."[5] Thus, it had a beginning and an end (cf. Heb. 9:9-10). It was added "until the Seed...had come." This Seed is Christ:

> *...The Scripture does not say "and to seeds," meaning many people, but "and to your seed," meaning one person, who is Christ. (Gal. 3:16)*

Therefore, the law was not God's permanent answer to man's need – it was only given as a temporary measure.

> *...For if a law had been given that could impart life, then righteousness would certainly have come by the law. But the Scripture declares that the whole world is a prisoner of sin, so that what was promised,*

---

[5] The Mosaic Covenant was "added" to the covenant of grace that God had previously made with Abraham. Thus, from God's side, His commitment to Israel – made to Abraham – would never be broken, even if Israel did not obey the Mosaic covenant of law (Lev. 26:42). God promised to remember the unconditional commitments He made to the Patriarchs (Deut. 4:31). In Galatians 3:17-18, Paul declares that God's promise to Abraham was not set aside by the introduction of the new covenant of the law. Thus, from God's side, His promise of grace remained in effect toward Israel, and in spite of Israel's failure to keep the law, they could not annul God's commitment to Abraham (Rom. 11:28-29). Since God's unconditional promise to Israel through Abraham stood firm, He provided a way for the forgiveness of their sins and the changing of their hearts, and their ultimate restoration to Himself through grace and on the basis of the New Covenant in the blood of Jesus Christ. Please see *An Introduction to the Older Testament* by Malcolm Webber, Lesson 8, for an extensive discussion of the covenants of God.

> *being given through faith in Jesus Christ, might be given to those who believe. Before this faith came, we were held prisoners by the law, locked up until faith should be revealed. So the law was put in charge to lead us to Christ that we might be justified by faith. Now that faith has come, we are no longer under the supervision of the law. (Gal. 3:21-25)*

The law was only for the time "before this faith came…until faith should be revealed." Therefore, "now that faith has come, we are no longer under the supervision of the law."

If it was only temporary, why did God give the law in the first place? Paul anticipated this very question in Galatians:

> *What, then, was the purpose of the law?… (Gal. 3:19)*

There are several reasons why God gave the law to Israel.

Why Was the Law Given?

God did not give the Law of Moses to Israel so that His people could be saved by obeying it. He gave the law for other reasons:

- God gave the law to reveal sin.
- By revealing his sinfulness, the law also exposed man's inability to save himself and thus his desperate need for a Savior.
- God gave Israel the law to foreshadow many aspects of the Person and work of the Messiah through whom sin would be dealt with and salvation offered to humanity.
- To some extent, the law restrained sin.
- God gave the law to preserve Israel.

Not for Man's Salvation

It must be carefully understood that God did not give the law to save man.

There is a common idea among Christians that God gave Israel the law as His means for their salvation. In reality, God Himself states that the law cannot possibly save man:

> *Be it known unto you therefore, men and brethren, that through this man is preached unto you the forgiveness of sins: And by him all that believe are justified from all things, from which ye could not be justified by the Law of Moses. (Acts 13:38-39)*

> *Now then, why do you try to test God by putting on the necks of the disciples a yoke that neither we nor our fathers have been able to bear? (Acts 15:10)*

> *...no one will be declared righteous in his sight by observing the law... (Rom. 3:20)*

> *...what the law could not do in that it was weak through the flesh... (Rom. 8:3, NKJV)*

> *...by observing the law no one will be justified. (Gal. 2:16)*

> *For as many as are of the works of the law are under the curse... that no one is justified by the law in the sight of God is evident, for "the just shall live by faith." Yet the law is not of faith, but "the man who does them shall live by them." (Gal. 3:10-12)*

> *...if a law had been given that could impart life, then righteousness would certainly have come by the law. (Gal. 3:21)*

> *The former regulation is set aside because it was weak and useless (for the law made nothing perfect), and a better hope is introduced, by which we draw near to God. (Heb. 7:18-19)*

In the Old Testament, God's people were not saved because they kept the law.[6] They were saved by their faith:

> *Abram believed the Lord, and he credited it to him as righteousness. (Gen. 15:6; see also Gal. 3:6)*

David also, along with all the other righteous men and women in the Old Testament, was saved by his faith:

> *David says the same thing when he speaks of the blessedness of the man to whom God credits righteousness apart from works: "Blessed are they whose transgressions are forgiven, whose sins are covered. Blessed is the man whose sin the Lord will never count against him." (Rom. 4:6-8)*

> *...the righteous will live by his faith (Hab. 2:4; see also Heb. 11)*

All the Old Testament saints were saved by grace through faith; they were not saved by law through their own works.

No one has ever been saved by keeping the law and no one ever will be. The law was not given to save man. God had other purposes in giving the law. There are several reasons why God gave the law to Israel.

---

[6] Theoretically, if someone kept the law they would have been saved by it (Lev. 18:5; Rom. 2:13b; 7:10; 10:5). But no one could ever keep it – all men are sinful by nature and by choice (1 Kings 8:46; Ps. 14:3; 51:5; Rom. 3:23).

To Reveal Sin

First, God gave the law to reveal sin.

Before the law was given, there was no transgression of the law.

> ... *where there is no law there is no transgression.* (Rom. 4:15)

There *was* sin and all its perpetrators came under its curse of death:

> *All who sin apart from the law will also perish apart from the law...* (Rom. 2:12)

> *Therefore, just as sin entered the world through one man, and death through sin, and in this way death came to all men, because all sinned* (Rom. 5:12)

Man's sin always was violating the holiness of God. However, it was not a formal "transgression" of the law.

> *For until the law sin was in the world, but sin is not imputed [as a transgression] when there is no law.* (Rom. 5:13, NKJV)

Consequently, God gave the law to reveal sin. When the law came, it gave a new meaning to sin – it became a transgression of the law.

> *Therefore no one will be declared righteous in his sight by observing the law; rather, through the law we become conscious of sin.* (Rom. 3:20)

The law was not given to make men righteous but to make men conscious that they were sinners and therefore subject to the wrath of God upon their sin.

> *What shall we say, then? Is the law sin? Certainly not! Indeed I would not have known what sin was except through the law. For I would not have known what coveting really was if the law had not said, "Do not covet." (Rom. 7:7)*

The law does not cause man to sin, but it reveals man's actions as sinful by giving God's evaluation of them. The law brings full accountability.

> *So then, the law is holy, and the commandment is holy, righteous and good. Did that which is good, then, become death to me? By no means! But in order that sin might be recognized as sin, it produced death in me through what was good, so that through the commandment sin might become utterly sinful. We know that the law is spiritual; but I am unspiritual, sold as a slave to sin. (Rom. 7:12-14)*

In Romans 7, Paul states:

- "…I would not have known what sin was except through the law…" (v. 7).

- "…But in order that sin might be recognized as sin…" (v. 13).

- "…so that through the commandment sin might become utterly sinful" (v. 13).

The purpose of the law was to expose man's utter sinfulness. By virtue of his conscience, man always knew that he was sinning against God (Rom. 2:14-15), but when the law came, man's sin became "utterly sinful" (Rom. 7:13), his trespass "increased" (Rom. 5:20).

> *…the power of sin is the law. (1 Cor. 15:56)*

> *…the sinful passions aroused by the law… (Rom. 7:5)*

The law actually strengthens the power of sin over those who are under the law. The harder they strive to keep the law, the more conscious they become of the power of sin within themselves, exercising dominion over them, even against their own will (Rom. 7:14-24[7]), and frustrating their desire to live by the law.

> *The law was added so that the trespass might increase... (Rom. 5:20)*

This was not only for Israel's benefit. Israel's experience was to demonstrate to the whole world the desperate sinfulness of humanity.

> *Now we know that whatever the law says, it says to those who are under the law, so that every mouth may be silenced and the whole world held accountable to God. Therefore no one will be declared righteous in his sight by observing the law; rather, through the law we become conscious of sin. (Rom. 3:19-20)*

Thus, the purpose of the law was not to save man but to reveal his sinfulness, to bring sin out into the open and to expose it in all its hideousness. The sin had always been there, killing man. Now it is revealed!

The law became like a mirror to reveal the true condition of man. Without a mirror, man cannot see himself as he really is. But that is all a mirror can do – show man his own filthiness and his need for washing. The mirror cannot do the washing. If a man tried to use a mirror to take the dirt away, it would only make the situation worse by rubbing the dirt in and spreading it around! So too the law could only reveal man's sinfulness – it could not deliver man from his sin. For that, man needed a savior.

---

[7] In the author's view, the latter verses of Romans 7 refer to Paul's struggle, as a devout religious man, *before* he found Christ, when he tried unsuccessfully to obey the law that he loved and honored.

To Reveal Man's Need for a Savior

Second, by revealing his sinfulness, the law also exposed man's inability to save himself and thus his desperate need for a Savior.

> *So the law was put in charge to lead us to Christ that we might be justified by faith. (Gal. 3:24)*

There is a natural tendency in fallen man to try to be independent of God. When a man realizes his flaws, his first reaction is often to try to cure himself of his sinful condition and make himself righteous by his own efforts, without falling upon the grace and mercy of God. Indeed, many religious Israelites did this:

> *Since they did not know the righteousness that comes from God and sought to establish their own, they did not submit to God's righteousness. (Rom. 10:3)*

Israel did not submit to God; His purpose in giving them the law was to show them, not that they *could* obey it and thus establish their own righteousness, but that they could *not* obey it and therefore desperately needed a Savior.

To Reveal the Coming Messiah

Third, God gave Israel the law to foreshadow many aspects of the Person and work of the Messiah through whom sin would be dealt with and salvation offered to humanity.

This was done in two main ways:

1. Direct prophecy revealed the coming Messiah who would bring salvation and righteousness to His people.

> *Philip found Nathanael and told him, "We have found the one Moses wrote about in the Law, and about whom the prophets also wrote – Jesus of Nazareth, the son of Joseph." (John 1:45)*

There are many such direct prophecies in the Old Testament (Gen. 3:15; Deut. 18:18-19; Ps. 23; Is. 53; etc.). Jesus Himself referred to them:

> *You diligently study the Scriptures because you think that by them you possess eternal life. These are the Scriptures that testify about me, yet you refuse to come to me to have life. (John 5:39-40)*

> *He said to them, "How foolish you are, and how slow of heart to believe all that the prophets have spoken! Did not the Christ have to suffer these things and then enter his glory?" And beginning with Moses and all the Prophets, he explained to them what was said in all the Scriptures concerning himself. (Luke 24:25-27)*

> *He said to them, "This is what I told you while I was still with you: Everything must be fulfilled that is written about me in the Law of Moses, the Prophets and the Psalms." Then he opened their minds so they could understand the Scriptures. (Luke 24:44-45; see also Heb. 10:5-7)*

2. The Messiah was foreshadowed through the types of the law.[8]

> *The law is only a shadow of the good things that are coming – not the realities themselves… (Heb. 10:1)*

---

[8] Please see *The Blood of God* by Malcolm Webber, chapters 10 and 11 for an extensive discussion of this.

> *Therefore do not let anyone judge you by what you eat or drink, or with regard to a religious festival, a New Moon celebration or a Sabbath day. These are a shadow of the things that were to come; the reality, however, is found in Christ. (Col. 2:16-17)*

> *The next day John saw Jesus coming toward him and said, "Look, the Lamb of God, who takes away the sin of the world!" (John 1:29)*

The tabernacle, the priesthood, the sacrifices, the feasts, the holy days, the ordinances, and the rituals all foreshadow Christ typologically in many ways.

Thus, the law was given to Israel to expose man's sinfulness, his inability to establish his own righteousness and his desperate need for a Savior, and also to reveal the coming Messiah who would save man from his sin and bring true righteousness.

These purposes of the law are summed up by Paul in Galatians:

> *Therefore the law was our tutor to bring us to Christ, that we might be justified by faith. (Gal. 3:24, NKJV)*

The word "tutor" refers to a senior slave in the household of a wealthy man, who had the responsibility to give the first stages of instruction to his master's children and to escort them each day to and from school. It was the tutor's duty to never lose sight of his charge in public, to prevent association with objectionable companions and to instill moral lessons at every opportunity. The tutor had this responsibility until the child reached maturity.

In the same way, the law was given to Israel to bring her to the Messiah. It was only temporary; the law was not intended by God to save Israel, but to bring her to faith in Christ. Just as the tutor's task was complete when the boy became of age and was accepted into the family with full liberty and privileges as a son of the father, so the law's task was complete once it had brought Israel to her Messiah:

> But after faith has come, we[9] are no longer under a tutor. (Gal. 3:25, NKJV)

To Restrain Sin

The law cannot save man from his sin, but it does have the effect of restraining man somewhat in his sin through the fear of punishment.

> ...We also know that law is made not for the righteous but for lawbreakers and rebels, the ungodly and sinful, the unholy and irreligious; for those who kill their fathers or mothers, for murderers, for adulterers and perverts, for slave traders and liars and perjurers – and for whatever else is contrary to the sound doctrine that conforms to the glorious gospel of the blessed God, which he entrusted to me. (1 Tim. 1:9-11)

God intended the law to restrain sin in Israel, thus setting her apart from her idolatrous and wicked neighbors.

> Keep all my decrees and laws and follow them, so that the land where I am bringing you to live may not vomit you out. You must not live according to the customs of the nations I am going to drive out before you. Because they did all these things, I abhorred them. But I said to you, "You will possess their land; I will give it to you as an inheritance,

---

[9] Paul is speaking to Gentiles here, but says that "we" (meaning the Jews) are no longer under the law.

*a land flowing with milk and honey." I am the L*ORD *your God, who has set you apart from the nations. You must therefore make a distinction between clean and unclean animals and between unclean and clean birds. Do not defile yourselves by any animal or bird or anything that moves along the ground – those which I have set apart as unclean for you. You are to be holy to me because I, the L*ORD*, am holy, and I have set you apart from the nations to be my own. (Lev. 20:22-26)*

To Preserve Israel

Finally, God gave the law to preserve Israel. This final purpose of the law is also spoken of by Paul in Galatians:

But before faith came, we were kept under guard by the law, kept for the faith which would afterward be revealed. (Gal. 3:23, NKJV)

The law kept Israel as a special nation, set apart from all others by her distinctive rituals and laws. God's intention was that Israel be "a people who live apart and do not consider themselves one of the nations" (Num. 23:9).

Even though Israel's disobedience caused her to be scattered among the nations, the Jews have remained a distinct element within other cultures. They have never completely lost their identity as a people. The main instrument in this has been their continued identification with the Law of Moses.

In summary, the law was never given to save man from his sin. The law was given to reveal man's sin and his need for a Savior. This was not only for Israel's benefit; Israel's experience was to demonstrate to the whole world the desperate sinfulness of humanity. Then the law revealed the coming Savior. While Israel was waiting for her Messiah who would save her from her sin, the law restrained her sin. When the Messiah came, His people rejected him and were scattered among the nations; nevertheless, they retain their distinct identity as a people by virtue of the Law of Moses as God prepares them to receive the Messiah at His Second Coming.

All these purposes were only temporary:

> *Now that faith has come, we are no longer under the supervision of the law. (Gal. 3:25)*

All these purposes were fulfilled in Christ:

> *Christ is the end of the law so that there may be righteousness for everyone who believes. (Rom. 10:4)*

Thus, the law was not God's ultimate purpose for His people, but it was only to lead Israel to her Messiah. We will now examine the Messiah's own relationship to the law.

Jesus' Relationship to the Law

Jesus' attitude and relationship to the law are summed up by His own words in the Sermon on the Mount:

> *Do not think that I have come to abolish the Law or the Prophets; I have not come to abolish them but to fulfill them. (Matt. 5:17)*

Jesus did not disregard the law but He fulfilled it in several ways:

- He was born under the law.
- He perfectly kept the law.
- He fulfilled the prophecies contained in the law.
- He honored the law.

- His death vindicated the law.
- His death abolished the law.

Born Under the Law

First, Jesus was born under the law:

> But when the time had fully come, God sent his Son, born of a woman, born under law, to redeem those under law, that we might receive the full rights of sons. (Gal. 4:4-5)

Jesus Christ was born as a Jew, subject to all the obligations of the law. As a Child, He was circumcised on the eighth day and consecrated to God (Luke 2:21-24, 39). Every year He celebrated the Feast of the Passover with His parents (Luke 2:41-42). Jesus was brought up in the instruction of the law (Luke 2:46-47, 52).

Kept the Law

Second, as an adult, Jesus continued to perfectly obey the law:

> For we do not have a high priest who is unable to sympathize with our weaknesses, but we have one who has been tempted in every way, just as we are – yet was without sin. (Heb. 4:15; see also 5:7-9; 7:26; 2 Cor. 5:21; 1 Pet. 2:22; Is. 53:9, 11; 1 John 3:5; John 14:30)

Jesus perfectly kept both the letter and the spirit of the law.

Fulfilled the Prophecies Contained in the Law

Third, as we have already noted in the previous chapter, Jesus perfectly fulfilled all the prophecies about Himself contained in the law.

Honored the Law

Fourth, even when correcting the self-righteous legalism of the religious leaders, Jesus always honored the law:

> *Woe to you, teachers of the law and Pharisees, you hypocrites! You give a tenth of your spices – mint, dill and cummin. But you have neglected the more important matters of the law – justice, mercy and faithfulness. You should have practiced the latter, without neglecting the former. (Matt. 23:23)*

> *I tell you the truth, until heaven and earth disappear, not the smallest letter, not the least stroke of a pen, will by any means disappear from the Law until everything is accomplished. Anyone who breaks one of the least of these commandments and teaches others to do the same will be called least in the kingdom of heaven, but whoever practices and teaches these commands will be called great in the kingdom of heaven. For I tell you that unless your righteousness surpasses that of the Pharisees and the teachers of the law, you will certainly not enter the kingdom of heaven. (Matt. 5:18-20)*

Jesus' Death

Finally, since man could never be saved by the law, Jesus died on the cross to fulfill the law's requirements for the punishment of man's sin and to make a way open for man's salvation. Thus, Jesus' death on the cross both vindicated and abolished the law.

The Cross and the Law

By Jesus' death, He both vindicated and abolished the law. Paul expresses this clearly in Romans:

> Do we, then, nullify the law by this faith? Not at all! Rather, we uphold the law. (Rom. 3:31)

As we have seen, the law revealed man's sin and the fact that man cannot be saved by keeping the law (Rom. 3:20; 7:13; etc.). The law was never given to save man. Therefore, the fact that salvation is by God's grace received through faith both abolishes the law for the believer (since righteousness can only come as a free gift from God and can not be earned by our works) *and* vindicates the law (since the law performed its appointed task by clearly revealing the sinfulness of man and the impossibility of righteousness by works and thus leading man to his Savior).

Furthermore, as we will see, those who are in Christ will fulfill the "righteous requirements of the law" (Rom. 8:1-4). Out of their love for God and the reality of their new lives in Christ they will live in righteousness and truth.

Thus, through Jesus' death on the cross the law was validated and "upheld" (Rom. 3:31), and, happily for the believer, the law was also abolished:

> *having abolished in His flesh the enmity, that is, the law of commandments contained in ordinances... (Eph. 2:15, NKJV)*

The Greek word translated "abolished" in Ephesians 2:15 means to render inactive or inoperative, to put out of use.[10] Thus, this verse does not imply that the law *itself* no longer exists (cf. Matt. 5:18), but that *for the believer* the law has been entirely set aside.

> *having canceled the written code, with its regulations, that was against us and that stood opposed to us; he took it away, nailing it to the cross. (Col. 2:14)*

The Greek word translated "canceled" in Colossians 2:14 means to completely erase or wipe out. The figure is the erasure of hand-writing. The law is completely gone for the Christian; it is taken away, having been nailed to the cross. The literal Greek meaning of "took it away" is "out of the midst." The law is no longer "in the midst," in the foreground, as debtor's obligation is constantly before him, accusing him. The law with its moral demands was abolished in Christ's death, as if crucified with Him. The law was given through Moses as a single, complete system, and as a single, complete system it was abolished at the cross.

---

[10] The same verb is used in Hebrews 2:14 where the devil is said to be "destroyed." Obviously Satan himself still exists but his power over Christians' lives was broken by Jesus' death on the cross (cf. 2 Tim. 1:10 – Christ also "destroyed" death).

> *Christ is the end of the law so that there may be righteousness for everyone who believes. (Rom. 10:4)*
>
> *The former regulation is set aside because it was weak and useless (for the law made nothing perfect), and a better hope is introduced, by which we draw near to God. (Heb. 7:18-19)*
>
> *If perfection could have been attained through the Levitical priesthood (for on the basis of it the law was given to the people), why was there still need for another priest to come – one in the order of Melchizedek, not in the order of Aaron? For when there is a change of the priesthood, there must also be a change of the law. (Heb. 7:11-12)*
>
> *…He sets aside the first to establish the second. (Heb. 10:9)*

Jesus did not abolish the law in the sense of disregarding or ignoring it, but He did abolish the law for the believer by fulfilling it. Consequently, the Christian is free from the law.

The Christian and the Law

In previous sections, we examined four key facts:

1. The Law of Moses was only ever given to Israel. The Mosaic Covenant was never intended for the Gentiles.

2. The law was one single, complete system.

3. The law was intended by God to be only temporary.

4. The law was abolished at the cross.

In view of these truths, the relationship of the Christian to the law becomes very clear: the righteousness of the Christian does not depend upon observing the law or any part of it.

Free from the Law

The New Testament makes it abundantly clear that the believer is free from the law. The believer is not only free from the penalty of the law but he is also free from the obligation to keep it.

> *But now a righteousness from God, apart from law, has been made known, to which the Law and the Prophets testify. This righteousness from God comes through faith in Jesus Christ to all who believe. There is no difference, for all have sinned and fall short of the glory of God, and are justified freely by his grace through the redemption that came by Christ Jesus. (Rom. 3:21-24)*

The law itself testified to this righteousness obtained through grace by faith.

> *For we maintain that a man is justified by faith apart from observing the law. (Rom. 3:28)*

> *For sin shall not be your master, because you are not under law, but under grace. (Rom. 6:14)*

> *What then? Shall we sin because we are not under law but under grace? By no means! (Rom. 6:15)*

> *So, my brothers, you also died to the law through the body of Christ, that you might belong to another, to him who was raised from the dead, in order that we might bear fruit to God. (Rom. 7:4)*

The believer is dead to the law. The law has as much jurisdiction over him as it does over a dead man.

> *But now, by dying to what once bound us, we have been released from the law so that we serve in the new way of the Spirit, and not in the old way of the written code. (Rom. 7:6)*

> *For through the law I died to the law so that I might live for God. (Gal. 2:19)*
>
> *Now that faith has come, we are no longer under the supervision of the law. (Gal. 3:25)*
>
> *But if you are led by the Spirit, you are not under law. (Gal. 5:18)*

Such verses reveal that Christians are not under the law but under grace. These are two mutually-exclusive alternatives. A person who is under grace is not under the law; no person can be under both the law and grace at the same time.[11]

> *What then shall we say that Abraham, our forefather, discovered in this matter? If, in fact, Abraham was justified by works, he had something to boast about – but not before God. What does the Scripture say? "Abraham believed God, and it was credited to him as righteousness." Now when a man works, his wages are not credited to him as a gift, but as an obligation. However, to the man who does not work but trusts God who justifies the wicked, his faith is credited as righteousness. David says the same thing when he speaks of the blessedness of the man to whom God credits righteousness apart from works: "Blessed are they whose transgressions are forgiven, whose sins are covered. Blessed is the man whose sin the Lord will never count against him." (Rom. 4:1-8)*
>
> *It was not through law that Abraham and his offspring received the promise that he would be heir of the world, but through the righteousness that comes by faith. For if those who live by law are heirs, faith has no value and the promise is worthless, (Rom. 4:13-14)*

---

[11] Please see the Appendix for a summary of the key differences between law and grace.

> *The law is not based on faith; on the contrary, "The man who does these things will live by them." (Gal. 3:12)*

> *For if the inheritance depends on the law, then it no longer depends on a promise; but God in his grace gave it to Abraham through a promise. (Gal. 3:18)*

Thus, those who are saved by grace cannot be under the law.

> *Christ is the end of the law so that there may be righteousness for everyone who believes. (Rom. 10:4)*

Christ is both the aim of the law and its termination. When a person puts his faith in Christ, that is "the end of the law" for that person as a means of achieving righteousness. The believer's righteousness is no longer derived from keeping the law, either wholly or in part, but solely from faith in Christ. Righteousness is not earned by the believer; it is given to him by God.

> *For if, by the trespass of the one man, death reigned through that one man, how much more will those who receive God's abundant provision of grace and of the gift of righteousness reign in life through the one man, Jesus Christ. (Rom. 5:17)*

> *God made him who had no sin to be a sin offering for us, so that in him we might become the righteousness of God. (2 Cor. 5:21, NIV margin)*

We are not saved through our own obedience to the law, but "through the obedience" of Christ:

> *Consequently, just as the result of one trespass was condemnation for all men, so also the result of one act of righteousness was justification that brings life for all men. For just as through the disobedience of the*

one man the many were made sinners, so also through the obedience of the one man the many will be made righteous. (Rom. 5:18-19)

Our righteousness is "by faith from first to last" (Rom. 1:17). It is by faith from the beginning to the end!

As we have seen, the law as a means of righteousness came to an end with the death of Jesus on the cross:

When you were dead in your sins and in the uncircumcision of your sinful nature, God made you alive with Christ. He forgave us all our sins, having canceled the written code, with its regulations, that was against us and that stood opposed to us; he took it away, nailing it to the cross. (Col. 2:13-14)

Through Jesus' death, God "canceled the written code, with its regulations, that was against us and that stood opposed to us; He took it away, nailing it to the cross." It is very significant that Paul does not speak here about *sins* being canceled,[12] but about *the law itself* being canceled. The "written code, with its regulations" denotes the whole system of law which God gave through Moses, including the Ten Commandments. This was "canceled" for the believer at the cross.

That this "canceling" includes the Ten Commandments is confirmed by Paul two verses later:

Therefore do not let anyone judge you by what you eat or drink, or with regard to a religious festival, a New Moon celebration or a Sabbath day. These are a shadow of the things that were to come; the reality, however, is found in Christ. (Col. 2:16-17)

---

[12] Elsewhere, of course, the Bible does say that our sins are canceled (Col. 2:13; Eph. 4:32; 1 John 1:7, 9; etc).

The word "therefore" indicates a direct connection with the canceling of "the written code, with its regulations" that Paul just mentioned. The Christian should not allow anyone to judge him with regard to these observances *because* they were canceled at the cross through the death of Christ. The mention of the "Sabbath day" at the end of this verse indicates that the religious observance of the Sabbath was included among the "regulations" that were "canceled." The commandment to observe the Sabbath was the fourth of the Ten Commandments (Ex. 20:8-11). This indicates that the law in its entirety was "nailed to the cross."[13]

In 2 Corinthians 3:6-11, Paul declares that the part of the law that was written on stones (specifically the Ten Commandments) has been done away. Thus, he explicitly labels the "moral part" of the law as that which "kills" (v. 6), a "ministry that brought death" (v. 7), a "ministry that condemns men" (v. 9). This ministry he says has now been replaced by the New Covenant that brings life and righteousness.

As already observed, the law was a single, complete system. It was introduced as a single, complete system by Moses; and, as a single, complete system, it was done away with by Christ.

> *For he himself is our peace, who has made the two one and has destroyed the barrier, the dividing wall of hostility, by abolishing in his flesh the law with its commandments and regulations. His purpose was to create in himself one new man out of the two, thus making peace, and in this one body to reconcile both of them to God through the cross, by which he put to death their hostility. (Eph. 2:14-16)*

---

[13] Some Christians make a distinction between the "Law of Moses" and the "Law of the Lord," saying that the Law of Moses was canceled at the cross, but the Law of the Lord (the Ten Commandments) was not. This distinction is entirely inaccurate. The two terms are used interchangeably in Scripture (e.g., Luke 2:22-24, 39).

The Law of Moses was the great dividing line that separated the Jews from the Gentiles. Now Christ has "destroyed the barrier... by abolishing in his flesh [i.e. through His death] the law with its commandments and regulations." Thus it is now possible for Jews and Gentiles alike, through faith in Christ, to be reconciled both with God and with each other. Clearly the believer is not under the law or any part of the law. For the Christian, the law has been "abolished" in its entirety.

> *So, my brothers, you also died to the law through the body of Christ, that you might belong to another, to him who was raised from the dead, in order that we might bear fruit to God. For when we were controlled by the sinful nature, the sinful passions aroused by the law were at work in our bodies, so that we bore fruit for death. But now, by dying to what once bound us, we have been released from the law so that we serve in the new way of the Spirit, and not in the old way of the written code. (Rom. 7:4-6)*

> *For through the law I died to the law so that I might live for God. I have been crucified with Christ and I no longer live, but Christ lives in me. The life I live in the body, I live by faith in the Son of God, who loved me and gave himself for me. I do not set aside the grace of God, for if righteousness could be gained through the law, Christ died for nothing! (Gal. 2:19-21)*

> *It is for freedom that Christ has set us free. Stand firm, then, and do not let yourselves be burdened again by a yoke of slavery. Mark my words! I, Paul, tell you that if you let yourselves be circumcised, Christ will be of no value to you at all. Again I declare to every man who lets himself be circumcised that he is obligated to obey the whole law. You who are trying to be justified by law have been alienated from Christ; you have fallen away from grace. (Gal. 5:1-4)*

> *But if you are led by the Spirit, you are not under law. (Gal. 5:18; see also 4:21-31)*

The Jerusalem Council settled this matter early and clearly in Acts 15. Debating the question of whether or not circumcision was necessary for salvation, the council declared an emphatic no:

> *Now then, why do you try to test God by putting on the necks of the disciples a yoke that neither we nor our fathers have been able to bear? No! We believe it is through the grace of our Lord Jesus that we are saved, just as they are. (Acts 15:10-11)*

We do not have to keep the law – in whole or in part – to be righteous before God. We are saved by grace through faith.

This raises the question: If the Christian is not under the law, then are we free to break the law?

New Life in Christ

We have seen that salvation is received by the grace of God through faith alone – completely apart from keeping the law or any of its parts. The Christian is not under the law. But does this mean that the Christian can continue to live in sin and still be saved in the end?

In answer to this question, the Scriptures state that the believer who has been justified by faith, apart from the works of the law, will live in such a way as to fulfill the righteousness of the law.

> *For what the law could not do in that it was weak through the flesh, God did by sending His own Son in the likeness of sinful flesh, on account of sin: He condemned sin in the flesh, that the righteous requirement of the law might be fulfilled in us who do not walk according to the flesh but according to the Spirit. (Rom. 8:3-4, NKJV)*

The key phrase here is "the righteous requirement of the law." It is not the law itself that is to be fulfilled in Christians' lives, but the righteous requirement of the law. This is a vital distinction.

The Christian is not under the law. However, within the believer there is new life – God's holy life – and this new life will be expressed through the believer's life.

> *Therefore, if anyone is in Christ, he is a new creation; the old has gone, the new has come! (2 Cor. 5:17)*

> *What shall we say, then? Shall we go on sinning so that grace may increase? By no means! We died to sin; how can we live in it any longer? Or don't you know that all of us who were baptized into Christ Jesus were baptized into his death? We were therefore buried with him through baptism into death in order that, just as Christ was raised from the dead through the glory of the Father, we too may live a new life. (Rom. 6:1-4)*

The believer is not only dead to the law; he is also dead to sin. He has a new nature in the holy image of God:

> *and have put on the new self, which is being renewed in knowledge in the image of its Creator. (Col. 3:10)*

The Old Testament also speaks of this (Rom. 3:21):

> *I will give you a new heart and put a new spirit in you; I will remove from you your heart of stone and give you a heart of flesh. And I will put my Spirit in you and move you to follow my decrees and be careful to keep my laws. (Ezek. 36:26-27)*

> *"The time is coming," declares the LORD, "when I will make a new covenant with the house of Israel and with the house of Judah. It will*

not be like the covenant I made with their forefathers when I took them by the hand to lead them out of Egypt, because they broke my covenant, though I was a husband to them," declares the LORD. "This is the covenant I will make with the house of Israel after that time," declares the LORD. "I will put my law in their minds and write it on their hearts. I will be their God, and they will be my people." (Jer. 31:31-33)

Thus, the "righteous requirement of the law" will be fulfilled in the Christian. He will live in a manner consistent with the holy nature of God of which the Law of Moses was an expression.

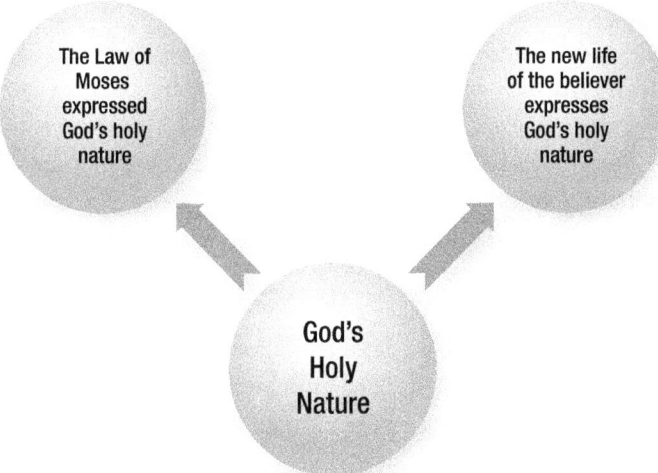

Although the Christian is not under the law, he has been given new life.

...every good tree bears good fruit...(Matt. 7:17)

When he lives according to this new life, the believer will live in a manner consistent with the nature of God, of which the Law of Moses was an expression.

> *But now, by dying to what once bound us, we have been released from the law so that we serve in the new way of the Spirit, and not in the old way of the written code. (Rom. 7:6)*

> *There is therefore now no condemnation to those who are in Christ Jesus, who do not walk according to the flesh, but according to the Spirit. (Rom. 8:1, NKJV)*

When God gave Israel the Law of Moses, it was not merely an arbitrary set of rules, but it was an expression of God's own nature, of His holiness, of His righteousness. Moreover, it was an expression of His love:

> *One of them, an expert in the law, tested him with this question: "Teacher, which is the greatest commandment in the Law?" Jesus replied: "'Love the Lord your God with all your heart and with all your soul and with all your mind.' This is the first and greatest commandment. And the second is like it: 'Love your neighbor as yourself.' All the Law and the Prophets hang on these two commandments." (Matt. 22:35-40)*

The Law of Moses was a detailed outworking of these two great commandments – love for God and love for one's neighbor. Thus, the law of love is the great law behind all other laws. Paul says this in Romans:

> *Let no debt remain outstanding, except the continuing debt to love one another, for he who loves his fellowman has fulfilled the law. The commandments, "Do not commit adultery," "Do not murder," "Do not steal," "Do not covet," and whatever other commandment there may be, are summed up in this one rule: "Love your neighbor as yourself." Love does no harm to its neighbor. Therefore love is the fulfillment of the law. (Rom. 13:8-10)*

The Christian is free from the law. But the man who is truly saved will walk in the newness of life that God has placed within him. This new life will naturally be expressed in love for God and love for other men.

> *If you obey my commands, you will remain in my love, just as I have obeyed my Father's commands and remain in his love. I have told you this so that my joy may be in you and that your joy may be complete. My command is this: Love each other as I have loved you. (John 15:10-12)*

> *For you, brethren, have been called to liberty; only do not use liberty as an opportunity for the flesh, but through love serve one another. For all the law is fulfilled in one word, even in this: "You shall love your neighbor as yourself." (Gal. 5:13-14, NKJV)*

> *I say then: Walk in the Spirit, and you shall not fulfill the lust of the flesh. (Gal. 5:16, NKJV)*

> *But the fruit of the Spirit is love, joy, peace, longsuffering, kindness, goodness, faithfulness, gentleness, self-control. Against such there is no law. And those who are Christ's have crucified the flesh with its passions and desires. If we live in the Spirit, let us also walk in the Spirit. (Gal. 5:22-25, NKJV)*

> *Carry each other's burdens, and in this way you will fulfill the law of Christ. (Gal. 6:2)*

> *If you really keep the royal law found in Scripture, "Love your neighbor as yourself," you are doing right. (Jam. 2:8)*

> *And this is his commandment, That we should believe on the name of his Son Jesus Christ, and love one another, as he gave us commandment. (1 John 3:23)*

As a result of the expression of his new life, the Christian will fulfill the righteous requirement of the law:

> *that the righteous requirement of the law might be fulfilled in us who do not walk according to the flesh but according to the Spirit. (Rom. 8:4, NKJV)*

In this way, the *grace* of God leads us into true holiness:

> *For the grace of God that brings salvation has appeared to all men. It teaches us to say "No" to ungodliness and worldly passions, and to live self-controlled, upright and godly lives in this present age, (Tit. 2:11-12)*

> *For we are God's workmanship, created in Christ Jesus to do good works, which God prepared in advance for us to do. (Eph. 2:10)*

> *But now he has reconciled you by Christ's physical body through death to present you holy in his sight, without blemish and free from accusation (Col. 1:22)*

> *let us draw near to God with a sincere heart in full assurance of faith, having our hearts sprinkled to cleanse us from a guilty conscience and having our bodies washed with pure water. (Heb. 10:22)*

Consequently, the Christian, although free from the law, will be enabled to live at a higher standard of holiness than those who attempt to keep the law:

> *For I tell you that unless your righteousness surpasses that of the Pharisees and the teachers of the law, you will certainly not enter the kingdom of heaven. (Matt. 5:20)*

Those who are alive to God will live in ways consistent with "the righteous requirements of the law" (Rom. 8:4).

Conversely, those who continue in sin will not see the eternal kingdom of God, no matter how much they reassure themselves that they are saved by God's grace and not by their own works.[14]

> *Every tree that does not bear good fruit is cut down and thrown into the fire. (Matt. 7:19)*
>
> *Not everyone who says to me, "Lord, Lord," will enter the kingdom of heaven, but only he who does the will of my Father who is in heaven. Many will say to me on that day, "Lord, Lord, did we not prophesy in your name, and in your name drive out demons and perform many miracles?" Then I will tell them plainly, "I never knew you. Away from me, you evildoers!" (Matt. 7:21-23; cf. 2 Pet. 2:18-22)*
>
> *Now the works of the flesh are evident, which are: adultery, fornication, uncleanness, lewdness, idolatry, sorcery, hatred, contentions, jealousies, outbursts of wrath, selfish ambitions, dissensions, heresies, envy, murders, drunkenness, revelries, and the like; of which I tell you beforehand, just as I also told you in time past, that those who practice such things will not inherit the kingdom of God. (Gal. 5:19-21, NKJV)*
>
> *For of this you can be sure: No immoral, impure or greedy person – such a man is an idolater – has any inheritance in the kingdom of Christ and of God. Let no one deceive you with empty words, for*

---

[14] We should not think of grace as being "sloppier" than the law or as having a more casual approach to lifestyle. Anyone who rejected the Law of Moses died without mercy on the testimony of two or three witnesses; anyone who knows and then rejects the grace of God will face much more severe punishment (Heb. 2:2-3; 10:28-29; 12:25).

because of such things God's wrath comes on those who are disobedient. Therefore do not be partners with them. (Eph. 5:5-7; cf. 1 John 3:6-10)

Put to death, therefore, whatever belongs to your earthly nature: sexual immorality, impurity, lust, evil desires and greed, which is idolatry. Because of these, the wrath of God is coming (Col. 3:5-6)

Essentially Equivalent Terms

The matter becomes quite clear when we realize that the following expressions are essentially equivalent to each other, expressing the same reality of new life in Christ from different angles:

- Called "to the obedience that comes from faith" (Rom. 1:5).
- "Live a new life" (Rom. 6:4).
- "Alive to God in Christ Jesus" (Rom. 6:11).
- "Offer yourselves to God, as those who have been brought from death to life" (Rom. 6:13).
- "Slaves to righteousness" (Rom. 6:18).
- "Offer [your body] in slavery to righteousness leading to holiness (Rom. 6:19).
- "You have been set free from sin and have become slaves to God" (Rom. 6:22).
- "Serve in the new way of the Spirit" (Rom. 7:6).
- "Do not walk according to the flesh, but according to the Spirit" (Rom. 8:1, NKJV).
- Fulfill "the righteousness requirements of the law" (Rom. 8:4).
- "Live...according to the Spirit" (Rom. 8:4).
- "Your spirit is alive because of righteousness (Rom. 8:10).
- "Led by the Spirit of God" (Rom. 8:14).
- "If anyone is in Christ, he is a new creation; the old has gone, the new has come!" (2 Cor. 5:17).
- "Live for God" (Gal. 2:19).

- "Live by faith in the Son of God" (Gal. 2:20).
- You "have clothed yourself with Christ" (Gal. 3:27).
- "Live by the Spirit" (Gal. 5:16).
- "Keep in step with the Spirit" (Gal. 5:25).
- "Fulfill the law of Christ" (Gal. 6:2).
- "The one who sows to please the Spirit" (Gal. 6:8).
- "Keep the royal law" (Jam. 2:8).
- Bear "good fruit" (Matt. 7:17).
- "Remain in me, and I will remain in you" (John 15:4).
- "Those who obey his commands live in him, and he in them" (1 John 3:24).

The believer was once bound by sin; he was lost and condemned. Now he is made alive to God, having been united with Christ in His death and resurrection. Now he lives in union and communion with Christ. New life is in the believer's heart, and so he will now walk in a manner consistent with that new life. This new life will naturally express the holy nature of God, of which the Law of Moses was an expression.

Although saved by grace, the believer will not see this as an excuse for spiritual laziness or lack of initiative; in fact, he will be highly motivated to pursue loving God and his neighbor.

The Christian's Focus

If the Christian sees himself as still "under law" of some kind then he will naturally try to keep that law, and his life will be focused on trying to keep an externally-imposed commandment through his own ability and strength. Since he can't keep the law perfectly, his life will be characterized by ever-increasing self-effort, frustration and condemnation. He will continue in much the same struggle as Paul did before he was saved (Rom. 7:14-24).[15]

---

[15] Some Christians think that Paul is speaking of the *believer's* life in Romans

If, however, the Christian understands that he is not under the law – that he has, in fact, "died to the law" (Rom. 7:4; Gal. 2:19) – and that he is united with Christ in His resurrection and life, then his focus will be on living in inward union with Christ by His Spirit.

> *Remain in me, and I will remain in you. No branch can bear fruit by itself; it must remain in the vine. Neither can you bear fruit unless you remain in me. "I am the vine; you are the branches. If a man remains in me and I in him, he will bear much fruit; apart from me you can do nothing." (John 15:4-5)*

> *…those who live in accordance with the Spirit have their minds set on what the Spirit desires. (Rom. 8:5)*

The believer will not look at the law but at the face of Jesus Christ and as he looks he will be transformed.

> *…where the Spirit of the Lord is, there is liberty. But we all, with unveiled face, beholding as in a mirror the glory of the Lord, are being transformed into the same image from glory to glory, just as by the Spirit of the Lord. (2 Cor. 3:17-18, NKJV)*

> *…inwardly we are being renewed day by day. (2 Cor. 4:16)*

> *Since, then, you have been raised with Christ, set your hearts on things above, where Christ is seated at the right hand of God. Set your minds on things above, not on earthly things. For you died, and your life is now hidden with Christ in God. (Col. 3:1-3)*

7:14-24. In reality he is showing from his own experience as a well-taught Pharisee (Phil. 3:5) that the purpose of the law was to show that man (even a pious Jew like Paul who was instructed by and loved the law, cf. Rom. 2:18) cannot keep it and desperately needs a Savior (Rom. 7:24-25a). It is understandable that poorly-taught Christians who are trying to keep the law will experience the same frustration that Paul experienced, and will identify with his experience even though it was before he was saved.

> *Now this is eternal life: that they may know you, the only true God, and Jesus Christ, whom you have sent. (John 17:3)*

Thus, by the enabling power of the indwelling Spirit the believer will actually be able to live in victory and newness of life!

> *...how much more will those who receive God's abundant provision of grace and of the gift of righteousness reign in life through the one man, Jesus Christ. (Rom. 5:17)*

Not Just Semantics!

Some might ask: What is the difference between teaching people that they are obligated to keep the moral law and teaching people that they are inwardly changed and will therefore live in holiness? Won't the practical results of both teachings be the same?

Our answer is that this whole issue is not just semantics. The practical consequences of each of these two approaches are profoundly different! The following table details some of the dramatic contrasts between the two lifestyles.

	Law	**Grace**
Nature of the believer's life:	Obey the "moral law"	Union and communion with Christ (John 17:3)
Focus:	Self-effort (Gal. 3:3)	God's presence (John 15:5; Rom. 8:13; 2 Cor. 3:18)
Based on:	Religious man's belief that he actually can keep the law (Ex. 19:8)	Total dependence on Christ alone (John 15:4-5; Phil. 1:6; 2 Tim. 1:12)
Appropriate guides for the believer's life:	Commandments and regulations (Eph. 2:15; Col. 2:14)	Love God and your neighbor (Rom. 13:8-10; Gal. 6:2; 1 Cor. 9:21)
Immediate results:	Human labor, fleshly striving	Peace with God (Rom. 5:1) and all the fruits of the Spirit (Gal. 5:22-23)
Long-term results:	In God's eyes, the result will always be failure. However, if the individual incorrectly perceives success, the results will be pride and self-righteousness. If the individual accurately perceives failure, the results will be frustration, fear and condemnation.	Daily transformation from glory to glory into the image of Christ by the power of the Holy Spirit

In summary:

1. The Christian is free from the law in its entirety. He does not have to keep it to be righteous before God.

2. The Christian is also changed (2 Cor. 5:17). He has new life within him. United with Christ, the believer has died to sin and has risen to newness of life.

3. When he lives according to this new life, the believer will live in a manner consistent with the nature of God, of which the Law of Moses was an expression.

4. This new lifestyle is epitomized by love – love for God and love for one's neighbor.

5. Thus, the believer, while not obligated to "keep the law," will, nevertheless, fulfill the "righteous requirements of the law" and his righteousness will surpass that of the Pharisees.

6. The believer's ongoing focus should therefore not be on trying to obey an external law through his own carnal strength, but on seeking to love God and to walk in the Spirit through inward fellowship with Christ.

This accurate understanding of the Christian's relationship to the law will bring the believer into an abiding rest in Christ (Matt. 11:28-30) and will protect him from the terrible bondage of legalism.

Legalism

Broadly speaking, there are three kinds of legalism:

- We must keep the law to be saved by God.
- We are saved by faith but we must keep the law to go deeper with God.
- We must keep the law to be accepted by men.

To Be Saved by God

The first kind of legalism demands the strict observance of certain laws as necessary for salvation. Keeping the law, or parts of it, is seen as necessary for achieving and maintaining right standing with God. Thus, obedience to the rules wins divine favor and salvation.

This was the legalism of the Judaizers:

> *Some men came down from Judea to Antioch and were teaching the brothers: "Unless you are circumcised, according to the custom taught by Moses, you cannot be saved."... Then some of the believers who belonged to the party of the Pharisees stood up and said, "The Gentiles must be circumcised and required to obey the law of Moses." (Acts 15:1, 5)*

To Go Deeper With God

The second kind of legalism requires the practice of outward religious forms in order to "go deeper with God." Salvation is understood as being by faith alone, but obedience to certain outward forms brings greater holiness and deeper spirituality. This was the legalism of the false teachers at Colosse who attempted to introduce into the church certain mystical views and legalistic practices:

> *See to it that no one takes you captive through hollow and deceptive philosophy, which depends on human tradition and the basic principles of this world rather than on Christ... do not let anyone judge you by what you eat or drink, or with regard to a religious festival, a New Moon celebration or a Sabbath day. These are a shadow of the things that were to come; the reality, however, is found in Christ. (Col. 2:8, 16-17)*

> *Since you died with Christ to the basic principles of this world, why, as though you still belonged to it, do you submit to its rules: "Do not handle! Do not taste! Do not touch!"? These are all destined to perish with use, because they are based on human commands and teachings. Such regulations indeed have an appearance of wisdom, with their self-imposed worship, their*

false humility and their harsh treatment of the body, but they lack any value in restraining sensual indulgence. (Col. 2:20-23)[16]

To Be Accepted by Men

The third kind of legalism requires adherence to certain external moral codes in order to maintain right standing within a particular religious community. Obedience to the rules (whether explicit or implicit) wins human favor. This is the legalism of the religious groups today who have their own rules about what constitutes holiness of dress or behavior.

They want to be teachers of the law, but they do not know what they are talking about or what they so confidently affirm. (1 Tim. 1:7)

Such groups use external criteria to determine who is accepted in the group and who is not. These criteria tend to be highly visible and relatively superficial, and they frequently substitute for true inward holiness. So, for example, a pastor who is proud and resentful may remain in good standing in his church, but if he is ever caught smoking a cigarette he will be fired. This does not mean that anyone in the church would actually say that smoking is a worse sin than pride or resentment; smoking is simply a visible criterion that determines acceptability by the group.

These criteria can vary considerably from group to group. In a conservative Pentecostal church, women's dress or length of hair may be the issues. While in some churches the women have to wear dresses to be accepted, the author knows of other churches where women have to wear pants! In a "faith church," whether or not one maintains one's

---

[16] For a thorough analysis of these verses in Colossians 2, please see *The Preeminence and All-Sufficiency of Jesus Christ: A Brief Exposition of Colossians* by Malcolm Webber.

"positive confession" of faith for healing might determine his status of acceptance. In some Amish churches, whether or not one owns a car or uses electricity are the key issues of acceptance by their group.

Certainly, in the church we are to hold one another accountable but this accountability should concern issues of the heart and not mere externals (1 Cor. 5:1-13).

The Heart of Legalism

The essence of all three kinds of legalism is that one is trying to obey an externally-imposed requirement through his own strength to try to live up to a standard of some kind and to earn approval – either from God or from man.

In contrast, the essence of true righteousness is when one walks in inward union with Christ by His Spirit – free from the law – already accepted by God and accepting one another.

Christ has set us free! We should not allow ourselves to be brought back under the reign of the law in any form.

Consequently, all three forms of legalism should be vigorously resisted and confronted in our own lives and ministries.[17]

> *It is for freedom that Christ has set us free. Stand firm, then, and do not let yourselves be burdened again by a yoke of slavery. (Gal. 5:1)*

---

[17] God has called us to be responsible for our own lives and ministries. He may or may not give us the calling and authority to correct others for their errors (Rom. 14). When we are really free, then we can even submit ourselves to the wrong convictions of others for the purpose of reaching them with the truth (1 Cor. 9:19-23).

However, the Christian should not be ignorant of the law just because he is not under it.

The Appropriate Use of the Law

Although the Christian is not under the law, he should not be entirely ignorant of it.

> *But we know that the law is good, if a man use it lawfully;* (1 Tim. 1:8)

A Revelation of Truth and Righteousness

First, the law has an important place in the Christian community in that it gives us a clear revelation of righteousness for the purpose of instruction in the ways of God.

> *...in the law [is] the embodiment of knowledge and truth (Rom. 2:20)*

New Testament writers make frequent use of the law in various ways, affirming its underlying morality and applying its principles. Since it was an expression of God's holy nature, the teachings of the law reveal the appropriate outworkings of internal divine life.

> *Children, obey your parents in the Lord, for this is right. "Honor your father and mother" – which is the first commandment with a promise – "that it may go well with you and that you may enjoy long life on the earth." (Eph. 6:1-3)*

This statement does not indicate that Paul is retracting his own extensive teaching in Romans and Galatians (as well as Hebrews) that the believer is not under the law. For him there is no contradiction. The Christian is not under the law, but he is changed and new life within him will produce righteousness of lifestyle that is consistent with the righteousness of God of which the law was an expression. Thus, the law is a wonderful source of instruction in righteousness.

> *All Scripture [referring to the Old Testament] is God-breathed and is useful for teaching, rebuking, correcting and training in righteousness, so that the man of God may be thoroughly equipped for every good work. (2 Tim. 3:16-17)*

The law came from God. It reveals His truth, righteousness and love.

Here are more examples of how New Testament writers use the teachings of the law to instruct believers:

> *Anyone who breaks one of the least of these commandments and teaches others to do the same will be called least in the kingdom of heaven, but whoever practices and teaches these commands will*

be called great in the kingdom of heaven. For I tell you that unless your righteousness surpasses that of the Pharisees and the teachers of the law, you will certainly not enter the kingdom of heaven. (Matt. 5:19-20)

As in all the congregations of the saints, women should remain silent in the churches. They are not allowed to speak, but must be in submission, as the Law says. (1 Cor. 14:34)

As obedient children, do not conform to the evil desires you had when you lived in ignorance. But just as he who called you is holy, so be holy in all you do; for it is written: "Be holy, because I am holy." (1 Pet. 1:14-16 with Lev. 11:44-45)

The elders who direct the affairs of the church well are worthy of double honor, especially those whose work is preaching and teaching. For the Scripture says, "Do not muzzle the ox while it is treading out the grain," and "The worker deserves his wages." (1 Tim. 5:17-18)

Don't we have the right to food and drink?... Do I say this merely from a human point of view? Doesn't the Law say the same thing? For it is written in the Law of Moses: "Do not muzzle an ox while it is treading out the grain." Is it about oxen that God is concerned? Surely he says this for us, doesn't he?... Don't you know that those who work in the temple get their food from the temple, and those who serve at the altar share in what is offered on the altar? In the same way, the Lord has commanded that those who preach the gospel should receive their living from the gospel. (1 Cor. 9:4-14; see also 2 Cor. 13:1-2; 6:14-18; 1 Cor. 5:1-5, 13)

In using the law for Christian teaching we must avoid two extremes:

- Legalism. In using the law as a source of instruction we must be careful not to bring people under it.

- Weakness. We can be so afraid of bringing people under bondage to the law that we don't teach the Word of God with authority and conviction.

Our challenge is to balance teaching the Word of God with authority and conviction while not bringing the people under bondage to legalism. The following principles[18] will help:

- The teacher should be mature in his walk with God. He must not be under the law himself. If he is confused he will spread confusion to others.
- He should have a close fellowship with God and bear a good witness in his life. Authority comes from genuine relationship with God.
- The teaching should be done in love without condemnation. The teacher's genuine intention must be to help people grow and not merely to advance a religious agenda.
- The teacher should pray seriously for those he teaches. He should teach boldly but gently and with humility.
- Stress should be put on the inner change of one's life and not merely external issues.
- The truth should be taught from the whole counsel of God and not from isolated passages. It should be strengthened by what is revealed in the law; while the focus must always remain on Christ, not on the law.
- The teacher should teach with an understanding that it is God who changes people, not man. Therefore, resisting the temptation to try to force people into the religious mould of his own thinking, the teacher should strive to lead people to God by His Spirit; such teaching will set people free.
- The teacher should not demand immediate transformation but he should commit the people's growth to God, realizing

---

[18] These principles were shared by Asian church leaders during a teaching of this entire book.

that the renewal of the mind takes time. At the same time, he should teach with expectation and hope, knowing that the truth will bear fruit.

A Basis for Civil Jurisprudence

Second, the Law of Moses has an important place in secular society in general[19] as a basis for civil jurisprudence.

> *We know that the law is good if one uses it properly. We also know that law is made not for the righteous but for lawbreakers and rebels, the ungodly and sinful, the unholy and irreligious; for those who kill their fathers or mothers, for murderers, for adulterers and perverts, for slave traders and liars and perjurers – and for whatever else is contrary to the sound doctrine that conforms to the glorious gospel of the blessed God, which he entrusted to me. (1 Tim. 1:8-11)*

Though it cannot change the heart, civil law can to some extent inhibit lawlessness in a fallen world by its threats of judgment, especially when backed by a civil code that consistently administers punishment for offenses (Rom. 13: 1-7; Eccl. 8:11).

In this way the law secures a measure of civil order and goes some way to protect society from rampant evil.

Jewish Believers

Finally, it is appropriate for the law to still occupy a unique place in the lives of Jewish believers, as we will now see.

---

[19] Particularly in the Western world.

Jewish Believers and the Law

The law is a part of the culture and tradition of the Jew. It is not wrong therefore that he should continue to observe certain parts of it – as long as he does not do so to establish or maintain his righteousness before God.

Consider several passages in Acts that relate to Paul's observance of certain parts of the Mosaic law. Paul circumcised Timothy:

> *Paul wanted to take him along on the journey, so he circumcised him because of the Jews who lived in that area, for they all knew that his father was a Greek. (Acts 16:3)*

Paul took a vow himself:

> *Paul stayed on in Corinth for some time. Then he left the brothers and sailed for Syria, accompanied by Priscilla and Aquila. Before he sailed, he had his hair cut off at Cenchrea because of a vow he had taken. (Acts 18:18)*

He also purified himself and the Jews with him at Jerusalem:

> *The next day Paul took the men and purified himself along with them. Then he went to the temple to give notice of the date when the days of purification would end and the offering would be made for each of them. (Acts 21:26)*

Some have used these verses to try to prove that Paul "kept the law," and therefore we should "keep the law" too. However, whatever these passages in Acts mean, they could not mean that Paul "kept the law" or that he intended us to "keep the law." We know that because of the very clear statements Paul made in his letters that show we are definitely not "under the law" (Rom. 3:21; 6:14-15; 7:4-6; Eph. 2:15; Col. 2:14, 16-17; etc.). The testimony of the clear, repeated teachings of the New Testament is that we are not under the law. We do not have to keep it to be saved and we do not have to keep it to mature in holiness or spirituality.

When we consider the previous verses from Acts in the light of Paul's entire teaching, we see that Paul was not, in fact, "keeping the law" to be right with God. Instead, his actions were intended to maintain his witness before the Jews. His concern was that he and the Jewish brothers with him should not bring an unnecessary offense to the Jews by violating the traditions and customs of the Jewish people.

> *Paul wanted to take him along on the journey, so he circumcised him because of the Jews who lived in that area, for they all knew that his father was a Greek. (Acts 16:3)*

The context of Paul's purification in Acts 21:26 also makes this clear. Consider the previous verses:

> *The next day Paul and the rest of us went to see James, and all the elders were present. Paul greeted them and reported in detail what God had done among the Gentiles through his ministry. When they heard this, they praised God. Then they said to Paul: "You see, brother, how many thousands of Jews have believed, and all of them are zealous for the law. They have been informed that you teach all the Jews who live among the Gentiles to turn away from Moses, telling them not to circumcise their children or live according to our customs. What shall we do? They will certainly hear that you have come, so do what we tell you. There are four men with us who have made a vow. Take these men, join in their purification rites and pay their expenses, so that they can have their heads shaved. Then everybody will know there is no truth in these reports about you, but that you yourself are living in obedience to the law. (Acts 21:18-24)*

Thus Paul's concern was not to "keep the law" before God, but to keep the law before man – in the sense of maintaining the Jewish customs and traditions. It was not a theological issue for Paul but a practical issue of ministry strategy.

> *To the Jews I became like a Jew, to win the Jews. To those under the law I became like one under the law (though I myself am not under the law), so as to win those under the law. (1 Cor. 9:20)*

> *So whether you eat or drink or whatever you do, do it all for the glory of God. Do not cause anyone to stumble, whether Jews, Greeks or the church of God – even as I try to please everybody in every way. For I*

> am not seeking my own good but the good of many, so that they may be saved. Follow my example, as I follow the example of Christ. (1 Cor. 10:31 – 11:1)

Significantly, Paul *refused* to circumcise Titus (Gal. 2:3-5).[20] Titus was a Gentile and in this case the gospel as freedom for Gentiles was at stake. In Paul's mind, circumcision of a man with Jewish heritage for ministry among Jews (Timothy) and circumcision of a Gentile in order to have right standing with God as a believer (Titus) were two radically different things!

Even the Gentiles in the book of Acts (who were never considered "under the law" in the first place; cf. Ps. 147:19-20; Rom. 3:2) were instructed to live in such a way so as to not bring unnecessary offense to the Jews:

> *...we should not make it difficult for the Gentiles who are turning to God. Instead we should write to them, telling them to abstain from food polluted by idols, from sexual immorality, from the meat of strangled animals and from blood. For Moses has been preached in every city from the earliest times and is read in the synagogues on every Sabbath.* (Acts 15:19-21)[21]

However, while it is appropriate to abstain from certain practices to avoid unnecessary offense to the Jews, Gentiles should be careful not to fall into the trap of placing themselves under the law or any of its parts.

---

[20] Moreover, Paul told the (Gentile) Galatians that if they were circumcised, they would lose their very salvation (Gal. 5:1-4)!

[21] Significantly, the Gentiles were *not* told here that they had to keep the Ten Commandments. It would have been the perfect place to affirm such an obligation had it been appropriate.

Specific Issues

Gentiles are free from the law. However, not every Christian believes that. Often, Gentile believers will consider themselves still obligated to obey certain parts of the law. We have already dealt with the idea that we are under the Ten Commandments. After that, the most common issues involve:

- Sabbath observance.
- Tithing.
- Dietary laws.

The logic that is usually given is that these religious institutions were initiated by God before the law was given; therefore they are an ongoing obligation for the believer in spite of the fact that the law was abolished for the believer at the cross.

Sabbath Observance

The word Sabbath is applied to several religious festivals in the Law of Moses, but principally and usually it refers to the seventh day of the week. In that sense, Sabbath observance was initiated by God Himself at the time of creation (Gen. 2:2-3). At Sinai, the Sabbath was incorporated into the Law of Moses, becoming the fourth commandment (Ex. 20:8-11; Deut. 5:12-15). The Sabbath was to be a day of rest (Ex. 20:10) and spiritual observance (Lev. 24:5-8; Num. 28:9-10).

In addition to the seventh-day Sabbath, the law also included other Sabbaths:

- Day of Atonement (Lev. 16:31; 23:32).
- Feast of Trumpets (Lev. 23:24).
- Feast of Tabernacles (Lev. 23:39).
- The seventh year was a sabbatical year when the fields had a rest from cultivation and the debts of fellow Israelites were remitted (Lev. 25:2-7; Ex. 23:10-11; Deut. 15:1-18).
- After every series of seven sabbatical years, the fiftieth year was observed as a year of Jubilee, when property reverted to its original owner and Israeli servants regained their freedom (Lev. 25:8-54).

With the rest of the Law of Moses, all these Sabbaths were abolished for the believer at the cross of Jesus Christ:

> *When you were dead in your sins and in the uncircumcision of your sinful nature, God made you alive with Christ. He forgave us all our sins, having canceled the written code, with its regulations, that was against us and that stood opposed to us; he took it away, nailing it to the cross... Therefore do not let anyone judge you by what you eat or drink, or with regard to a religious festival, a New Moon*

celebration or a Sabbath day. These are a shadow of the things that were to come; the reality, however, is found in Christ. (Col. 2:13-17)

Notice that Paul specifically mentions that we are no longer under obligation to keep the Sabbath or the other religious festivals. Those laws were all "nailed to the cross."

But now that you know God – or rather are known by God – how is it that you are turning back to those weak and miserable principles? Do you wish to be enslaved by them all over again? You are observing special days and months and seasons and years! I fear for you, that somehow I have wasted my efforts on you. (Gal 4:10-11)

Significantly, the decrees of the council of Jerusalem made no mention of sabbath-keeping in their requirements for the Gentile believers (Acts 15:28ff).

Furthermore, the early church met on the first day of the week and not on the seventh, Sabbath day:

On the first day of the week we came together to break bread… (Acts 20:7; see also 1 Cor. 16:2)

This was the day of Jesus' resurrection and is called the "Lord's Day" (Rev. 1:10).

While the duty of keeping the Sabbath as a religious observance was nailed to the cross, we still need to rest – physically, mentally and emotionally. This was the spiritual principle contained in the original law (Rom. 8:4). Jesus told us we need to rest:

Then, because so many people were coming and going that they did not even have a chance to eat, he said to them, "Come with me by yourselves to a quiet place and get some rest." (Mark 6:31)

Here is the meaning of spiritual rest for the believer. It is much deeper than merely not doing anything physical and watching television all day. That is not true "rest." In our weekly times of rest we should stop and look: backward, upward and ahead.

- Backward: we should pause and reflect on the past week and consider its meaning and purpose.
- Upward: we should get before God and allow Him to reveal the motives of our hearts and bring alignment with His will and purpose. This should be a time of returning to eternal truths, sorting out the truths and commitments by which we are living, recalibrating our spirits, reaffirming what we believe and why we do what we do. This should be done through praying, reading, meditating and reflecting.
- Forward: We should look at what is coming in the future and meditate on its potential problems, opportunities and possibilities. Moreover, we should define our mission: looking to the future, affirming our intentions to pursue a Christ-centered tomorrow, pondering where we are headed in the coming days, defining our intentions and making our dedications.

That is the spiritual meaning of weekly rest for the believer. It should not revolve around the legalistic questions of whether or not a believer is permitted to mow his lawn or wash his car on Sunday, or which day is the "right one to observe," but the heart issue is a spiritual pursuit of God, a clarification of His will for one's life, and a rejuvenating by His Spirit of one's life.

Consequently, for the godly Christian, freedom from the obligation of Sabbath observance will not result in the believer trying to maintain three full-time jobs and destroying himself and his family through overwork; it will produce a deeper and clearer relationship with God.

In summary, although he does need to rest, the Christian is free from having to maintain the Sabbaths and the other holy days and festivals of the Law of Moses.

Tithing

Tithes in Israel consisted of one-tenth of all yearly produce and of the increase of flocks and cattle. This was declared to be sacred to the Lord (Lev. 27:30-33). There were other tithes in the law such as the festival tithe (Deut. 12:5-6, 17-18) and the triennial tithe (Deut. 14:28-29; 26:12-15).

Tithing was practiced before the law was given, although it was not established as a formal duty. Abraham tithed to Melchizedek (Gen. 14:20) and Jacob made a vow to tithe to God (Gen. 28:22). Then tithing was a part of the law given to Moses.

Tithing, along with the rest of the law, was nailed to the cross (Col. 2:14; Eph. 2:15). Accordingly, the New Testament does not instruct the Christian believer to tithe. To declare that the Christian will come under a curse if he does not dutifully tithe (e.g., Mal. 3:6-12) is to attempt to bring him under the law from which God has delivered him.

However, the righteous principle contained in the original law of tithing will still be fulfilled in the Christian's life (Rom. 8:4). In recognition that everything he owns is a gift from God (1 Chron. 29:14),[22] the believer will give back to God a part of his increase. This giving should be:

---

[22] To teach, as some tithing proponents do, that ten percent of one's income belongs to God while the rest belongs to the believer is ludicrous. It all belongs to God (1 Cor. 6:19-20)! Significantly, the Pharisees gave tithes to God (Matt. 23:23), but they did not give Him all their hearts (cf. Matt. 5:20)!

- An act of worship (Matt. 2:11); an expression of our love for God and our surrender to Him. In the Old Testament law, tithing was an act of worship.
- Both private (Matt. 6:1-4) and public (Acts 4:34-37; 2 Cor. 8:24).
- Regular (1 Cor. 16:2). Giving should be a regular discipline whether we feel "anointed to give" or not. In addition we should give during crises as well as other special times.
- Proportional (1 Cor. 16:2). We give the "firstfruits" of what God has given us.
- Joyful (2 Cor. 9:7; Matt. 13:44). We should not give because we have to, but because we want to.
- Without compulsion (2 Cor. 9:7).
- According to what we have (2 Cor. 8:11-12). We should give out of what we have (cf. Mark 14:8; Luke 21:3-4) and not go into debt in order to give.
- Liberal (2 Cor. 9:6-11). The firstfruits is the best of the crop (cf. Mal. 1:6-14). We should give sacrificially (Luke 21:1-4; 2 Cor. 8:2).
- From the heart (2 Cor. 9:7).
- Expectant. As we sow we will reap (2 Cor. 9:6-11). God honors our obedience with His blessing (Prov. 3:9-10; 22:9; Luke 6:38; Phil. 4:17, 19).

Any idea of tithing for the believer is explicitly contradicted by Paul's instructions to the Corinthians:

Remember this: Whoever sows sparingly will also reap sparingly, and whoever sows generously will also reap generously. Each man should give what he has decided in his heart to give, not reluctantly or under compulsion, for God loves a cheerful giver. (2 Cor. 9:6-7)

First, Paul says that the believer should give "what he has decided in his heart to give." Clearly this rules out the common idea of tithing, which is a set ten percent.[23]

Second, Paul says our giving should not be "under compulsion." Thus, we are not under the law. It is our privilege to give back to God a proportion of what He has given us.

Thus, a giving Christian is a healthy one:

- Giving is the nature of Christianity.

    ...they gave themselves first to the Lord and then to us in keeping with God's will...But just as you excel in everything – in faith, in speech, in knowledge, in complete earnestness and in your love for us – see that you also excel in this grace of giving... For you know the grace of our Lord Jesus Christ, that though he was rich, yet for your sakes he became poor, so that you through his poverty might become rich. (2 Cor. 8:5, 7, 9)

    You have been saved to serve (Gal. 5:13). If you are a Christian, then you are a giver. If you are selfish, are you really a Christian (1 John 3:16-19)?

- Giving brings strength.

    A believer who does not embrace the privilege of giving and the responsibility of sacrificing to support the work of God, will be a weak Christian. If he is inactive in giving, he will likely be inactive also in evangelism as well as in every other aspect of ministry. Weakness and passivity will pervade his life. Through

---

[23] It is certainly acceptable for a believer to determine in his heart that he will give ten percent of his income to the Lord (as both Abraham and Jacob did in Genesis). However, this must not be made into a law of tithing.

letting others take financial responsibility for the church, he will learn to accept the position of a passive recipient who relies on others instead of making every effort to supply his own needs. Instead of being a "giver" (Acts 20:35) he will become a "taker." Alternatively, a believer who gives will be dedicated and wholehearted in his self-giving commitment to the church family.

- A giving Christian provides for fruitful ministry.

If we close our hearts to God and keep everything to ourselves, we guarantee that the work of God will not go forward.

- A giving Christian will be a blessed Christian.

We should act in obedience to God's Word, whether or not we think we can afford to give. If we do not give when we have a little, it will be even harder for us to give when we have a lot. Moreover, the young believers at Philippi who gave "beyond their ability" and did so out of their own "extreme poverty" (2 Cor. 8:1-5) were the ones who received this promise from God:

> But my God shall supply all your need according to his riches in glory by Christ Jesus. (Phil. 4:19)

Thus, Christian giving is not out of duty or law, but it proceeds from the life of God in the believer's regenerated heart.

Dietary Laws

The idea of some animals being "clean" and others being "unclean" is found in Genesis in the time of Noah (Gen. 7:2, 8). This distinction then became part of the Law of Moses (Lev. 11:1-47) which was nailed to the cross:

When you were dead in your sins and in the uncircumcision of your sinful nature, God made you alive with Christ. He forgave us all our sins, having canceled the written code, with its regulations, that was against us and that stood opposed to us; he took it away, nailing it to the cross… Therefore do not let anyone judge you by what you eat or drink… These are a shadow of the things that were to come; the reality, however, is found in Christ. (Col. 2:13-17)

Since you died with Christ to the basic principles of this world, why, as though you still belonged to it, do you submit to its rules: "Do not handle! Do not taste! Do not touch!"? These are all destined to perish with use, because they are based on human commands and teachings. Such regulations indeed have an appearance of wisdom, with their self-imposed worship, their false humility and their harsh treatment of the body, but they lack any value in restraining sensual indulgence. (Col. 2:20-23)

We have the reality in Christ. We have the "better" covenant (Hebrews). Why should we go back to shadows? As Paul observes in Colossians 2, these shadows include religious dietary ordinances and prohibitions.

Thus, the Christian should not come under food laws. Paul's letter to Timothy predicts legalistic teachings related to food prohibitions:

The Spirit clearly says that in later times some will abandon the faith and follow deceiving spirits and things taught by demons. Such teachings come through hypocritical liars, whose consciences have been seared as with a hot iron. They forbid people to marry and order them to abstain from certain foods, which God created to be received with thanksgiving by those who believe and who know the truth. For everything God created is good, and nothing is to be rejected if it is received with thanksgiving, because it is consecrated by the word of God and prayer. (1 Tim. 4:1-5; see also Tit. 1:14-16)

Paul's words are clear: "everything God created is good, and nothing is to be rejected." Clearly, there are no food laws for the believer.

This does not mean that the Christian is obligated to eat everything! Certainly we are free to have our own personal likes and dislikes. Furthermore, we are free to avoid certain foods (such as "junk food") for health reasons. But, while avoiding certain foods may make us healthier, it will not make us holier!

It is clear throughout the New Testament that those who believe the gospel are freed from food laws:

> *Nothing outside a man can make him "unclean" by going into him. Rather, it is what comes out of a man that makes him "unclean." (Mark 7:15)*
>
> *...In saying this, Jesus declared all foods "clean." (Mark 7:19; see also Luke 11:40-41; Acts 10:9-16; 11:9)*

Significantly, the New Testament revelation is not only that the keeping of dietary laws is not necessary for righteousness, but that all foods are clean:

> *...Do not call anything impure that God has made clean. (Acts 10:15)*
>
> *For everything God created is good, and nothing is to be rejected if it is received with thanksgiving, (1 Tim. 4:4)*

Paul deals with food matters several other times (1 Cor. 10:23-33; Rom. 14:1–15:7; Col. 2:16-23). Each of these situations is different. Paul's overall guidelines regarding foods are:

1. Food has nothing to do with holiness:

   As one who is in the Lord Jesus, I am fully convinced that no food is unclean in itself... (Rom. 14:14)

   Therefore, one may eat or not eat as one may wish.

2. One who abstains from certain foods should not judge one who eats:

   ...the man who does not eat everything must not condemn the man who does, for God has accepted him. (Rom. 14:3; see also 1 Cor. 10:29-30)

3. One who is free to eat certain foods should respect the convictions of one who is not free to do so:

   The man who eats everything must not look down on him who does not...As one who is in the Lord Jesus, I am fully convinced that no food is unclean in itself. But if anyone regards something as unclean, then for him it is unclean. (Rom. 14:3, 14)

4. Those who formally demand abstinence from certain foods for religious or theological reasons should be opposed:

   Since you died with Christ to the basic principles of this world, why, as though you still belonged to it, do you submit to its rules: "Do not handle! Do not taste! Do not touch!"? These are all destined to perish with use, because they are based on human commands and teachings. Such regulations indeed have an appearance of wisdom, with their self-imposed worship, their false humility and their harsh treatment of the body, but they lack any value in restraining sensual indulgence. (Col 2:20-23)

> *Do not be carried away by all kinds of strange teachings. It is good for our hearts to be strengthened by grace, not by ceremonial foods, which are of no value to those who eat them. (Heb. 13:9; see also 1 Tim. 4:3-6)*

In the New Testament, holiness and purity ("cleanness") are viewed in internal spiritual terms rather than the outer ritual prescriptions of the law:

> *The blood of goats and bulls and the ashes of a heifer sprinkled on those who are ceremonially unclean sanctify them so that they are outwardly clean. How much more, then, will the blood of Christ, who through the eternal Spirit offered himself unblemished to God, cleanse our consciences from acts that lead to death, so that we may serve the living God! (Heb. 9:13-14)*

We are cleansed by Jesus' blood. Our purity is internal.

> *This is an illustration for the present time, indicating that the gifts and sacrifices being offered were not able to clear the conscience of the worshiper. They are only a matter of food and drink and various ceremonial washings – external regulations applying until the time of the new order. (Heb. 9:9-10; see also 10:1-4)*

The "external regulations" of food laws only applied "until the time of the new order."

The Whole Law Was Nailed to the Cross!

The promoters of all these observances declare that since these practices began before the law, they are still enduring obligations for the Christian. However, the practices of circumcision,[24] animal

---
[24] Gen. 17:9-27; 21:4; 34:14-24; Ex. 4:25-26.

sacrifice[25] and priesthood[26] also began before the law. Does this mean that they are enduring obligations for the believer?

All of these practices – Sabbath observance, circumcision, tithing, food laws, sacrifice and priesthood – became part of the Law of Moses, and the Law of Moses in its entirety was abolished at the cross when Jesus died.

> *by abolishing in his flesh the law with its commandments and regulations… (Eph. 2:15)*

Moreover, as we have seen, any person who comes under any part of the law is necessarily obligated to keep the whole law at all times.

> *It is for freedom that Christ has set us free. Stand firm, then, and do not let yourselves be burdened again by a yoke of slavery. Mark my words! I, Paul, tell you that if you let yourselves be circumcised, Christ will be of no value to you at all. Again I declare to every man who lets himself be circumcised that he is obligated to obey the whole law. You who are trying to be justified by law have been alienated from Christ; you have fallen away from grace. But by faith we eagerly await through the Spirit the righteousness for which we hope. For in Christ Jesus neither circumcision nor uncircumcision has any value. The only thing that counts is faith expressing itself through love. (Gal. 5:1-6)*

Consider Paul's evaluation of a "gospel" that added the works of the law to faith:

> *I am astonished that you are so quickly deserting the one who called you by the grace of Christ and are turning to a different gospel – which is really no gospel at all. Evidently some people are throwing*

---

[25] Abel in Gen. 4:4, Noah in Gen. 8:20-21, Job in Job 1:5, Abraham in Gen. 22:7, 13 and Jacob in Gen. 31:54.
[26] Gen. 14:18; Ps. 110:4; Job 1:5; 12:19; Heb. 5:10; 7:1-3.

> you into confusion and are trying to pervert the gospel of Christ. But even if we or an angel from heaven should preach a gospel other than the one we preached to you, let him be eternally condemned! As we have already said, so now I say again: If anybody is preaching to you a gospel other than what you accepted, let him be eternally condemned! (Gal. 1:6-9)

We have the final reality in Christ; we must never go back to the shadows!

Appendix

Key Differences between Law and Grace	
The covenant of law was given through Moses (John 1:17).	The covenant of grace was given to Abraham (Rom. 4:13; Gal. 3:16-17) and fulfilled in Christ (John 1:17).
The law only convicted men of transgressions showing them that they cannot be saved by works, but only by God's grace through faith (Gal. 3:19, 21-24; Rom. 3:20; 5:20; 7:13).	The grace of God promised the removal of sins (Gal. 3:18).
The law restrained and discouraged sin (Gal. 3:23-25).	Grace liberates man from sin's power (Rom. 6:1-14).
The law was parenthetical and temporary (Gal. 3:19, 23-25).	The covenant of grace is eternal (Gal. 3:17).
The law, as more alien and remote, was given through mediators – Moses representing the people before God, and the angels representing God before the people (Acts 7:53; Gal. 3:19; Heb. 2:2).	The grace of God is given directly and personally by God Himself in the Person of Jesus Christ (Gal. 3:25-27; see also John 1:17).
The law pointed to the Savior (John 1:45).	The grace of God provided the Savior (Col. 2:16-17).
The covenant of law had a fading glory (2 Cor. 3:7).	The covenant of grace has a greater and enduring glory (2 Cor. 3:8-11).
Anyone who rejected the law of Moses died without mercy on the testimony of two or three witnesses (Heb. 2:2; 10:28; 12:25).	Anyone who knows and then rejects the grace of God will face much more severe punishment (Heb. 2:3; 10:29; 12:25).

Strategic Press
www.StrategicPress.org

Strategic Press is a division of Strategic Global Assistance, Inc.
www.sgai.org

513 S. Main St. Suite 2
Elkhart, IN 46516
U.S.A

+1-844-532-3371 (LEADER-1)

www.ingramcontent.com/pod-product-compliance
Lightning Source LLC
Chambersburg PA
CBHW071738090426
42738CB00011B/2521